JUNGLE
BABIES
of the Amazon
Rain Forest

Pink River Dolphins

by Rachel Lynette

Consultant:
Dr. Mark C. Andersen
Department of Fish, Wildlife and Conservation Ecology
New Mexico State University

BEARPORT
PUBLISHING

New York, New York

Credits

Cover and Title, © Susan Montgomery/Shutterstock Images; 4–5, © Minden Pictures/
SuperStock; 6, © Red Line Editorial; 6–7, © guentermanaus/Shutterstock Images; 8,
© Red Line Editorial; 8–9, © Mark Carwardine/naturepl.com; 10–11, © Martin Camm
(WAC)/Red Line Editorial/naturepl.com; 10–11, © Rich Carey/Shutterstock Images
and © Martin Camm (WAC)/Red Line Editorial/naturepl.com; 11, © Evlakhov Valeriy/
Shutterstock Images; 12–13, © Minden Pictures/SuperStock; 14–15, © Minden Pictures/
SuperStock; 15, © FAUP/Shutterstock Images; 16–17, © NHPA/SuperStock; 18, © Minden
Pictures/SuperStock; 18–19, © NHPA/SuperStock; 20–21, © NHPA/SuperStock; 22 (top),
© guentermanaus/Shutterstock Images; 22 (middle), © Martin Camm (WAC)/Red Line
Editorial/naturepl.com and © Rich Carey/Shutterstock Images; 22 (bottom), © Janne
Hämäläinen/Shutterstock Images; 23 (top), © NHPA/SuperStock; 23 (middle), © FAUP/
Shutterstock Images; 23 (bottom), © Meryll/Shutterstock Images.

Publisher: Kenn Goin
Editor: Joy Bean
Creative Director: Spencer Brinker
Photo Researcher: Arnold Ringstad
Design: Emily Love

Library of Congress Cataloging-in-Publication Data

Lynette, Rachel.
  Pink river dolphins / by Rachel Lynette.
      pages. cm. — (Jungle babies of the Amazon rain forest)
  Includes bibliographical references and index.
  Audience: Ages 6-9.
  ISBN-13: 978-1-61772-758-0 (library binding)
  ISBN-10: 1-61772-758-X (library binding)
  1. Boto—Juvenile literature. I. Title.
  QL737.C436L96 2013
  599.53′809811—dc23
                                      2012039860

For more information, write to Bearport Publishing Company, Inc., 45 West 21st Street,
Suite 3B, New York, New York 10010. Printed in the United States of America.

10 9 8 7 6 5 4 3 2 1

Contents

Meet a baby pink river dolphin

A baby pink river dolphin swims with its mother.

The baby, called a calf, is always gray.

Some calves will turn pink as they get older.

Others will stay gray or turn light gray.

This is because not all pink river dolphins are pink.

4

mother

calf starting to turn pink

5

What is a
pink river dolphin?

Although they live in water, all dolphins are **mammals**—not fish.

Pink river dolphins have long, smooth bodies and long **beaks**.

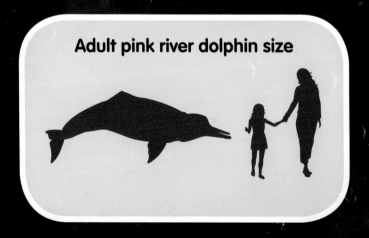

Adult pink river dolphin size

Inside their beaks are long rows of teeth.

The dolphins use their front teeth to hold their food.

They use their back teeth to chew food.

long beak

Where do pink river dolphins live?

Most dolphins live in salty ocean water.

Pink river dolphins do not.

They live only in **freshwater**.

The dolphins can be found in the lakes and rivers of South America's **rain forests**.

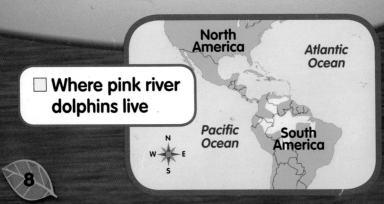

North America

Atlantic Ocean

☐ **Where pink river dolphins live**

Pacific Ocean

South America

N
W · E
S

rain forest

river

Special skill

The dolphins often live in muddy water, which makes it hard for them to see.

Fortunately, they have a special skill called **echolocation**.

To use the skill, a dolphin makes clicking sounds, which travel through the water.

When the sounds hit something, they bounce back toward the animal, like an echo.

Dolphins can tell the shape and distance of an object by listening to the echoes.

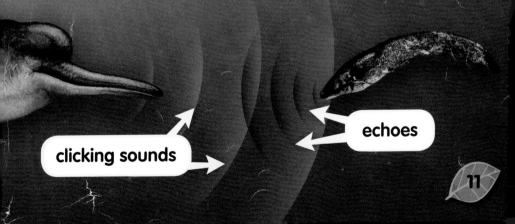

clicking sounds

echoes

Giving birth

Mother pink river dolphins give birth underwater.

They have only one calf at a time.

After her baby is born, the mother helps it swim to the surface for air.

She nudges her calf upward with her nose.

mother and calf swimming toward the surface

13

Growing up

For the first year of its life, a calf's only food is its mother's milk.

The rich milk helps the calf grow quickly.

mother swimming with calf

As it grows, the calf spends most of its time with its mother.

If **predators** such as sharks swim too close, the mother will protect her baby.

She will use her beak and flippers to scare away the enemies.

shark

Time to eat

Several times a year, pink river dolphins form groups that feed together.

They eat more than 40 different kinds of fish.

They also feed on river turtles and crabs.

In the groups, mothers and calves search for food together.

Some scientists believe pink river dolphin mothers teach their calves how to hunt.

Playtime

Pink river dolphins and their calves are playful animals.

They play with logs and sticks that float in the water.

They sometimes rub up against boats or even grab canoe paddles with their mouths.

dolphin playing with a floating seed

Playing helps the calves become better swimmers.

mother and calf playing with a leaf

19

All grown up

A pink river dolphin calf stays with its mother for two to three years.

After it leaves her, the grown-up calf lives alone.

Adult males live alone for their whole lives.

Adult females live alone until they give birth to calves of their own.

Then the cycle of life starts all over again.

adult
pink river
dolphin

Glossary

beaks (BEEKs)
hard, pointy mouth
parts used for eating

echolocation
(*ek*-oh-loh-KAY-shun)
a method for finding
an object's position by
sending out sounds that
bounce back to the sender

freshwater
(FRESH-wah-tur)
water that is not salty

mammals (MAM-uhlz)
warm-blooded animals
that have hair and
drink their mother's
milk as babies

predators (PRED-uh-turz)
animals that hunt and eat
other animals

rain forests
(RAYN for-ists)
large, warm areas of
land covered with trees
and plants, where lots
of rain falls

Index

Read more

Carney, Elizabeth. *Everything Dolphins.* Washington, DC: National Geographic Society (2012).

Seymour, Simon. *Dolphins.* New York: Collins (2011).

Stewart, Melissa. *Dolphins (National Geographic Readers).* Washington, DC: National Geographic Society (2010).

Learn more online

To learn more about pink river dolphins, visit
www.bearportpublishing.com/JungleBabies

About the author

Rachel Lynette has written more than 100 nonfiction books for children. She also creates resources for teachers. Rachel lives near Seattle, Washington. She enjoys biking, hiking, crocheting hats, and spending time with her family and friends.